The Hen
that Crowed

For Howard Weinberg and Alice Schertle, friends who help me do what I do — S.C.
For my mother the artist and my father the scientist — B.R.

First Edition   1 2 3 4 5 6 7 8 9 10

Library of Congress Cataloging in Publication Data. Cole; Sheila. The hen that crowed / by Sheila Cole: illustrated by Barbara Rogoff.   p.   cm.   Summary: Mr. Goodhart tries to stop his rooster from crowing, since roosters are illegal in the town of Bean Blossom, but his noisy bird's behavior ends up saving the town. ISBN 0-688-10112-7. — ISBN 0-688-10113-5 (lib. bdg.) [1. Roosters — Fiction.] I. Rogoff, Barbara, ill. PZ7.C67353He   1993   [E]—dc20 92-4907 CIP AC

The Hen that Crowed

by Sheila Cole ⟷ illustrated by Barbara Rogoff

Lothrop, Lee & Shepard Books / New York

In the old days, there were no roosters in Bean Blossom. There were chicks, and there were hens. But roosters were against the law. Everyone knows that at the first sign of light, roosters crow, *"Cock-a-doodle-doo. Time to wake up!"* And no one in Bean Blossom wanted to wake up at the first sign of light.

One day, Mr. Goodhart bought four chicks at the feed store.
"Hen chicks only, please," he told the clerk.

Hen chicks and rooster chicks look very much the same, but the clerk did what he could.

Mr. Goodhart named the chicks Henrietta, Geraldine, Clara, and Charlene. He liked their golden down. He liked the way they cheeped. And he especially liked the way they huddled together to go to sleep.

Day by day, the chicks grew bigger. Before long, feathers replaced their golden down. They were quickly turning from chicks into hens.

The first to lay an egg was Henrietta. She sat down on a pile of straw. *"Pawk-pawk,"* she said. When she got up, there was a small brown egg between her feet.

Next came Geraldine. *"Cluck-cluck,"* she said, and she laid an egg of her own.

"*Cackle-cackle,*" said Clara when she laid an egg in her nest.
But Charlene, the biggest of them all, did not lay an egg.
"Why don't you lay an egg?" the other chickens asked.
"What do you do?"
Charlene did not know.

She scratched in the dirt and ate the corn, and soon she began to change. A handsome red comb grew on her head. Proud sharp spurs grew on her legs. Beautiful green, black, and gold feathers grew in her tail.

And one morning, when the sun came up bright and

blazing over the hill, she suddenly knew what she did. Of course she didn't lay eggs! She was a he! And he did what roosters do. Charlene stretched out his neck and threw back his head. *"Cock-a-doodle-doo!"* he crowed. *"Time to wake up!"*

The crowing woke Mr. Goodhart, who sat straight up in bed. "That is a rooster," he said. "I cannot have a rooster. The neighbors will complain. He'll have to go into the soup."

Mr. Goodhart pulled on his overalls and stepped into his boots. He picked up his axe and marched out to the chicken coop.

But when Mr. Goodhart looked into Charlene's amber eyes, he could not bring himself to chop off the rooster's head. Instead, he took out his bandana and blindfolded him.

"Roosters do not know when to crow if they cannot see the sun rise," he said.

But Charlene was a rooster, and he was determined to do what roosters do. With his strong rooster feet, he tore the blindfold from his eyes. The hens all cheered. And when the sun came up over the hill, Charlene was ready. *"Cock-a-doodle-doo,"* he crowed. *"Time to wake up!"*

For the second time, Mr. Goodhart sat up straight in bed. "I *cannot* have a rooster," he said. "Roosters are against the law. He'll have to go into the soup."

But when Mr. Goodhart looked at Charlene's beautiful green, black, and gold tail feathers, he simply could not bring himself to do the cruel deed. Instead, he put the bird in a sack and tied it with a rope. "Roosters cannot stretch out their long necks, throw back their heads, and cock-a-doodle-doo in a sack," he said.

But Charlene was a rooster and he was determined to do what roosters do. While the hens pulled at the rope, he tore at the sack with his sharp spurs and ripped it with his strong beak.

When the sun came over the hill, Charlene stood tall, stretched out his neck, and threw back his head. *"Cock-a-doodle-doo,"* he crowed. *"Time to wake up!"*

For the third time, Mr. Goodhart sat straight up in his bed. "I cannot have a rooster!" he yelled. "The police will arrest me! He'll have to go into the soup!"

But when Mr. Goodhart saw Charlene's bright red comb, he could not bring himself to end that rooster's life. Instead, he locked Charlene in a dark shed. "Now no one will hear that rooster crow," he said.

But Charlene was a rooster, and he was as determined as ever to do what roosters do. He spotted a knothole high on a wall. His strong rooster wings carried him up to a beam. He sat there all day and looked out the hole, waiting for the sun to set.

He sat there all night, waiting for the sun to rise. At last, up on the hill, the light was bright and blazing. Then, just as he did every morning at the first light of day, Charlene crowed at the top of his lungs: *"Cock-a-doodle-doo, time to wake up!"*

Mr. Goodhart sprang out of bed. He glanced at his clock. One o'clock in the morning! "This is the last straw!" he bellowed. "That rooster will be soup tonight!"

But as Mr. Goodhart pulled on his overalls, he looked out his window. The sky was ablaze all right, but not with sunlight! Orange flames raced down the hill straight toward town. Yellow sparks flew into the sky. Smoke filled the air.

"Fire! Fire!" yelled Mr. Goodhart, but no one could hear him.

Everyone could hear Charlene, though. *"Cock-a-doodle-doo, time to wake up!"* Charlene crowed, and crowed again.

Before long, the whole town of Bean Blossom was awake and out of bed. The mayor, the librarian, and the chief of police all rushed to the scene. And so, of course, did the Bean Blossom Fire Brigade. Soon they put the fire out.

"Your rooster has saved our town!" said the chief of police, shaking Mr. Goodhart's hand.

"From now on, all roosters are welcome in Bean Blossom!" declared the mayor.

"Smile," said a photographer who took a picture for the *Bean Blossom Chronicle*.

As for Charlene? He continued to do what roosters do. Every morning at the first sign of light, he crowed, *"Cock-a-doodle-doo, time to wake up! Cock-a-doodle-doo, good morning to you!"*

19.14

Revised Edition

Michael
Phelps

By Jeffrey Zuehlke

AMAZING
ATHLETES

Lerner Publications Company/Minneapolis

Lerner Publications Company
A division of Lerner Publishing Group, Inc.
241 First Avenue North
Minneapolis, MN 55401 U.S.A.

Website address: www.lernerbooks.com

Library of Congress Cataloging in Publication Data

Zuehlke, Jeffrey, 1968–
    Michael Phelps / by Jeffrey Zuehlke. — Rev. ed.
       p.   cm. — (Amazing athletes)
    Includes bibliographical references and index.
    ISBN 978–0–7613–4055–3 (lib. bdg. : alk. paper)
    1. Phelps, Michael, 1985—Juvenile literature. 2. Swimmers—United States—Biography—Juvenile literature. I. Title.
    GV838.P54Z84 2009
    797.2'1092—dc22   2008040888

Manufactured in the United States of America
2 3 4 5 6 7 – BP – 14 13 12 11 10 09

TABLE OF CONTENTS

Michael dives into the pool for the 100-meter butterfly final at the 2008 Beijing Olympics.

GOING FOR THE GOLD

Michael Phelps was on a mission. He was competing at the 2008 Olympic Games in Beijing. He wanted to be the first Olympic athlete to win eight gold medals in the same Olympics. Michael had entered eight races. He had already won six golds. Every medal counted.

The seventh race—the final of the 100-meter butterfly—was the last one Michael would swim alone against other athletes. (The eighth and last race was a relay. He would share the job of racing with three other U.S. swimmers.)

Olympic-sized pools are 50 meters long. So in a 100-meter race, swimmers have to cross the pool twice. And in a 200-meter race, they cross it four times.

Knees bent, Michael waited on the starting block. "Hoooonk!" the starting buzzer sounded. Michael leaped into the water. He kept his legs together and pumped them like a flipper. After a few meters, he started doing the butterfly stroke. His long arms moved back and forth as he sped toward the end of the pool. On either side of him were seven other swimmers. Would Michael be good enough to beat them?

Michael *(bottom)* trails Serbian swimmer Milorad Cavic *(top)*.

If he could win one more medal, he would be the second person ever to win seven gold medals at one Olympic Games. (Another swimmer, Mark Spitz, was the first.)

Michael reached the end of the pool. He turned to swim the final lap. Even though he was trying hard, he was in seventh place. Michael spcd through the water like a shark. With only a little ways to go, Michael was

almost beside the lead swimmer, Milorad Cavic. Cavic stretched toward the wall. Michael was still too far away. He made a split-second decision. He took another half-stroke to try to reach the wall first. "When I took that last stroke, I thought I had lost," Michael said later.

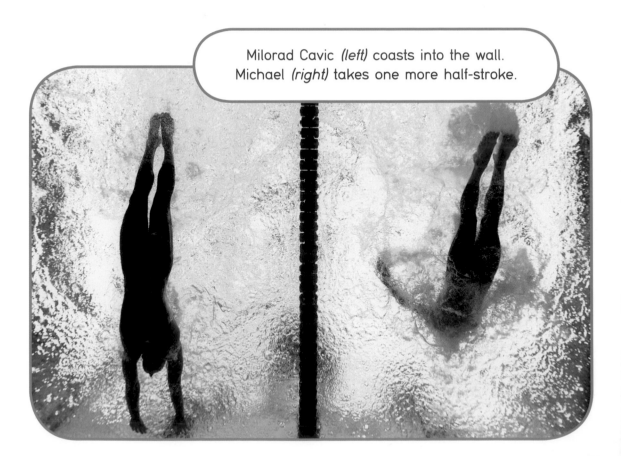

Milorad Cavic *(left)* coasts into the wall. Michael *(right)* takes one more half-stroke.

When his fingers touched the wall, Michael jumped up to look at the clock. He couldn't believe his eyes. He had beaten Cavic by one one-hundredth of a second. This is the smallest measurement in competitive swimming! Michael yelled with joy and started splashing around in the water. He had won seven gold medals. But what about getting the eighth gold to break the record?

Michael celebrates his victory in the 100-meter butterfly final.

Michael showed talent and focus at an early age.

AT HOME IN THE WATER

Michael Phelps was born on June 30, 1985, in Baltimore, Maryland. His mother, Debbie, was a teacher. His father, Fred, is a Maryland State Police officer. Michael's parents were divorced when he was in elementary school.

Michael grew up near Baltimore, Maryland.

Michael's two older sisters, Hilary and Whitney, are both talented swimmers. "My older sisters started the family in the sport of swimming," says Michael. "I grew up around the pool. . . . That was normal for me."

Michael joined the North Baltimore Aquatic Club (NBAC) team in 1992, when he was seven years old. He practiced swimming and competed in **meets** against other kids. Michael soon showed his talent for swimming.

In 1996, when Michael was eleven, he began working with a coach named Bob Bowman. Coach Bowman saw that Michael had a chance to be a great athlete. He encouraged Michael to work hard.

Michael has the perfect swimmer's body. He has long arms and big hands that can really move water. He also has short legs, which keep him from dragging in the water. Michael has big feet too. They work like dolphin flippers to move him through the water.

Michael began to practice twice a day, every day. "I swim seven days a week, two to five hours a day, about 50 miles a week," Michael says. "Once I'm in the water, I feel more at home."

Michael trained with NBAC's best athletes. Most of these swimmers were six or seven years older than Michael.

Before long, Michael began to catch up to the older swimmers. He won race after race. Some of these older swimmers didn't like losing to a young kid. "I got picked on some. . . . I would get frustrated. But it didn't do what they wanted, which I guess was to make me quit. It just made me swim faster."

Michael kept getting better. By 2000, fifteen-year-old Michael was already one of the best swimmers in the country. He was ready to try to achieve every swimmer's goal— to swim at the Olympic Games.

Michael's sister Hilary and his mother watch him win a race.

In 2000, Michael earned a spot on the U.S. Olympic Swim Team.

BOY WONDER

No one expected Michael to make the U.S. Olympic Swim Team. But he shocked everyone at the 2000 Olympic Trials. He swam great and earned a spot on the team. Michael was the youngest male swimmer to make the U.S. team in sixty-eight years!

At the 2000 Olympic Games in Sydney, Australia, Michael swam in the 200-meter butterfly event. He finished fifth, so he didn't earn a medal. He was disappointed but eager to get better.

His time in Sydney gave him a chance to watch some of the world's best swimmers. These swimmers included gold medalists Ian Thorpe of Australia and Pieter van den Hoogenband of the Netherlands. Michael wanted to be a superstar just like them.

Ian Thorpe (right) and Pieter van den Hoogenband watch the score clock after taking gold and silver in the 200-meter freestyle at the 2000 Olympic Games.

Michael swims the butterfly at the Sydney International Aquatic Center.

Michael kept training every day. He continued to improve. In early 2001, he set his first **world record**. He swam the best time ever in the 200-meter butterfly. Two years later, Michael set a world record in the 200-meter individual **medley**. Swimmers use a mixture of strokes in this type of race.

In July 2003, Michael competed in the World Championships in Barcelona, Spain. He broke *five* world records. He even set two world records on the same day! No one had ever done that before.

Just a few weeks later, he broke his own world record in the 200-meter individual medley. He had set seven world records in only a few months!

Suddenly, everyone was calling Michael the best swimmer in the world. But Michael didn't stop working hard. He set his sights on the 2004 Olympic Games. He was ready to make a big splash.

Michael watches the scoreboard at a race at the 2003 World Championships.

Michael seems relaxed at a news conference at the 2004 Olympic Games.

RACING IN ATHENS

Everyone knew Michael had a chance to win several medals at the 2004 Olympic Games. Some even thought he could break the record for the most gold medals at a single Olympics.

In 1972, U.S. swimmer Mark Spitz won seven gold medals. Could Michael top the great Mark Spitz?

Mark Spitz isn't jealous of Michael trying to break his record. "I'd like to see him do it," said Spitz.

Michael **qualified** for four individual events. He also hoped to swim in four relay events. "I want to break Mark Spitz's record," said Michael. "But if I can win one, just one [gold medal], I will consider these Olympics a success."

By the time the 2004 Olympic Games started, Michael was big news. His name and face were on magazine covers. He appeared on TV commercials and interviews. He was the most famous American at the Olympics. Everyone wanted to see if Michael could break Spitz's record. To do this, he would have to win gold in every event.

In his first race—the 400-meter individual medley—Michael won gold and set a new

world record. Next, he competed in the 4 × 100-meter **freestyle** relay. Michael's friend and teammate Ian Crocker was sick and had a bad race. Michael and his teammates settled for third place. The loss meant Michael wouldn't be able to break Spitz's record. But Michael didn't mind. He had already reached his goal of winning one gold medal.

Michael swims in the 400-meter individual medley.

His toughest race—the 200-meter freestyle—pitted him against Thorpe and van den Hoogenband. Many thought these two swimmers were among the all-time greats. Michael wanted to race against the best. In an exciting final, he came in third, after van den Hoogenband and Thorpe.

Michael still had five more events. He won four golds in the next few days. At this point, he had five gold medals and two bronze. The last **event** was the 4 × 100-meter medley relay. Each team can choose any four team members

Michael *(left)*, van den Hoogenband *(center)*, and Thorpe *(right)* race neck and neck for the gold in the 200-meter freestyle.

Gold medalist Michael (*left*) and silver medalist Ian Crocker pose after the 100-meter butterfly.

for the relay event. Michael was chosen to swim butterfly. But he gave up his spot to Ian Crocker. Crocker and the relay team went on to win. Because Michael had swum in the **prelims**, he was considered part of the relay team. So he got a gold medal too.

Michael had earned eight medals—six gold and two bronze. Before the Athens games had even ended, Michael was talking about the 2008 Olympic Games in Beijing. Would he take another shot at Spitz's record and history?

Michael swims the breastroke lap of the 400-meter individual medley final at the 2008 Olympics.

THE MICHAEL PHELPS OLYMPICS

Michael was proud of his success in Athens. But he knew he could do even better. Over the next four years, he trained every day. He broke world records in speed. He won national and international competitions. When the 2008

Olympic Games began, everyone was talking about Michael Phelps.

Michael got off to a golden start in the 400-meter individual medley. Even though he had a slow beginning, he beat the second-place swimmer by three whole seconds. As Michael accepted his gold medal, his eyes filled with tears.

Michael listens to the U.S. national anthem during the medal ceremony for his first gold medal in Beijing.

The next day, his team was competing in the 4 × 100 freestyle relay. Teammate Jason Lezak swam the anchor, or fourth, leg. But the U.S. team was behind. Michael's dream hinged on Lezak swimming the race of his life. Lezak came through, beating the French swimmer Alain Bernard by mere inches. Then Michael amazed everyone by shattering the world record time for the 200-meter freestyle. Michael and Team USA were on a roll.

Jason Lezak (left) trails the French team's Alain Bernard during the final length of the pool. Lezak swam a stunning race and caught up for the victory.

By the time he swam the 100-meter butterfly, Michael had six gold medals. His narrow victory over Milorad Cavic made it seven. Michael was the second person after Mark Spitz to win seven gold medals at one Olympic Games.

The 4 × 100 medley relay was the last event left for Michael. If the U.S. team won, he wouldn't just be tied with Spitz. He would have won more gold medals at a single Olympics than any athlete in history!

Michael swam the third part of the relay: the butterfly. When he dove into the water, the U.S. team was in third place. Michael swam faster than any of the other swimmers. When he climbed out of the pool, the Americans were in the lead. Lezak again helped his team finish the race in record time. And he helped Michael Phelps make Olympic history. When Michael saw the scoreboard, he shouted and hugged

From left: Michael and teammates Brendan Hansen, Jason Lezak, and Aaron Peirsol show off their gold medals from the 4 x 100-meter relay.

Michael hugs his mom and sisters after winning his eighth gold medal.

his teammates. "I couldn't have done it without you guys," he said. His mother and sisters had been in the stands for every win. He celebrated with them afterward.

People joked that the 2008 Olympics should be called the Michael Phelps Olympics. Michael knows that nothing is impossible. "With so many people saying it couldn't be done," he said, "all it took was a little imagination."

Michael poses with all eight of his gold medals from the 2008 Beijing Olympics.

What's next? Michael and Coach Bowman have said he wants to keep challenging himself as a swimmer. He also wants more people—especially kids—to get involved in his sport. And he's already looking toward the 2012 Summer Olympics in London, England. Go, Michael!

Selected Career Highlights

2008   Earned eight Olympic gold medals at the
Beijing Olympics: five in individual events and
three in relays
Broke four of his own world records
Broke the record for most Olympic gold medals
earned in a career and at a single Olympics

2007   Finished first in five events at the 2007 World
Championships
Set four individual world records at the 2007
World Championships

2006   Finished first in five events at the 2006 U.S. Nationals
Finished first in three events at the 2006 Pan Pacific Championships
Set a world record in two events at the 2006 Pan Pacific
Championships

2005   Finished first in two events at the 2005 World Championships
Finished first in two events at the 2005 U.S. Nationals

2004   Earned six Olympic gold medals at the Athens Olympics
Broke his own world record in the 400-meter individual medley
Set Olympic records in the 200-meter butterfly and 200-meter
individual medley

2003   Broke five world records at the 2003 World Championships in
Barcelona, Spain
Set a world record in the 200-meter butterfly at the World
Championships
Set world records twice in winning the 200-meter individual medley
at the 2003 World Championships

2001   Became the youngest male swimmer ever to break a world record

2000   Was the youngest male swimmer to make a U.S. Olympic team since
1932
Finished fifth in the 200-meter butterfly at the 2000 Olympic Games
in Sydney, Australia

Glossary

butterfly: a stroke in which the swimmer swims on his or her chest. The arms move together over and through the water. The legs kick together in a dolphin kick.

event: a race where swimmers compete in a stroke over a certain distance. For example, the 200-meter butterfly is an event in a swimming meet. An event can include prelims and finals.

final: the race that determines the winner of an event. Swimmers reach the final by doing well in the prelims and semifinals.

freestyle: a race in which swimmers can use any stroke they want. Freestyle swimmers today use the front crawl, the fastest stroke. In the front crawl, swimmers glide face down and pull their arms through the water one at a time. The legs kick separately, up and down.

gold medal: in the Olympics, the award for first place in an event. Second place receives a silver medal. Third place wins a bronze medal.

medley: an event in which a swimmer or a relay team swims a variety of strokes—the butterfly, the backstroke, the breaststroke, and freestyle

meets: gatherings where swimmers race one another

Olympic trials: a meet held a few months before each Olympic Games to determine who will make a country's Olympic team

prelims: short for preliminaries, the early races in a swim event. The best swimmers in the prelims go on to swim in the finals.

qualified: to have earned the right to swim in an event

relay: an event in which team members take turns swimming, one after the other. For example, in a 4 × 100-meter relay, each of four team members swim 100 meters.

starting block: a platform at the edge of the pool that a swimmer dives from at the start of a race

stroke: a certain style of swimming. For instance, the butterfly and the backstroke are swimming strokes.

world record: the fastest time ever recorded in an event

Further Reading & Websites

Christopher, Matt. *The Olympics: Legendary Sports Events*. London: Little, Brown, 2008.

Crossingham, John, Niki Walker, and Bobbie Kalman. *Swimming in Action*. New York: Crabtree, 2008.

Oxlade, Chris, and David Ballheimer. *Olympics*. New York: DK Publishing, 2005.

Page, Jason. *Swimming, Diving, and Other Water Sports*. New York: Crabtree, 2008.

The Official Website of the Olympic Movement
http://www.olympic.org/uk/sports/index_uk.asp
Learn more about the sport of swimming in this website's "Aquatics" section.

Sports Illustrated Kids
http://www.sikids.com
The *Sports Illustrated Kids* website covers all sports, including swimming and other Olympic events.

Index

Photo Acknowledgments

The images in this book are used with the permission of: © Timothy Clary/AFP/Getty Images, p. 4; AP Photo/Petr David Josek, p. 6; © Adam Pretty/Getty Images, p. 7; © Jamie Squire/Getty Images, p. 8; © Donald Miralle/Getty Images, p. 9; © Royalty-Free/CORBIS, p. 10; © Olivier Gauthier/DPPI/Icon SMI, pp. 12, 16; © Al Bello/Allsport/Getty Images, pp. 13, 14, 22, 23; © Ross Kinnaird/Allsport/Getty Images, p. 15; © Jeff Christensen/Reuters/CORBIS, p. 17; © Erich Schlegal/NewSport/Corbis, p. 19; © Icon SMI, p. 20; © Shaun Botterill/Getty Images, p. 21; AP Photo/Bob Bukaty, pp. 24, 25; AP Photo/Mark Baker, p. 26; AP Photo/Tom Curley, p. 27; © Al Bello/Octagon/Getty Images, p. 28; © David Gray/Reuters/Corbis, p. 29.

Front cover: © Mike Hewitt/Getty Images.

JB PHE
924

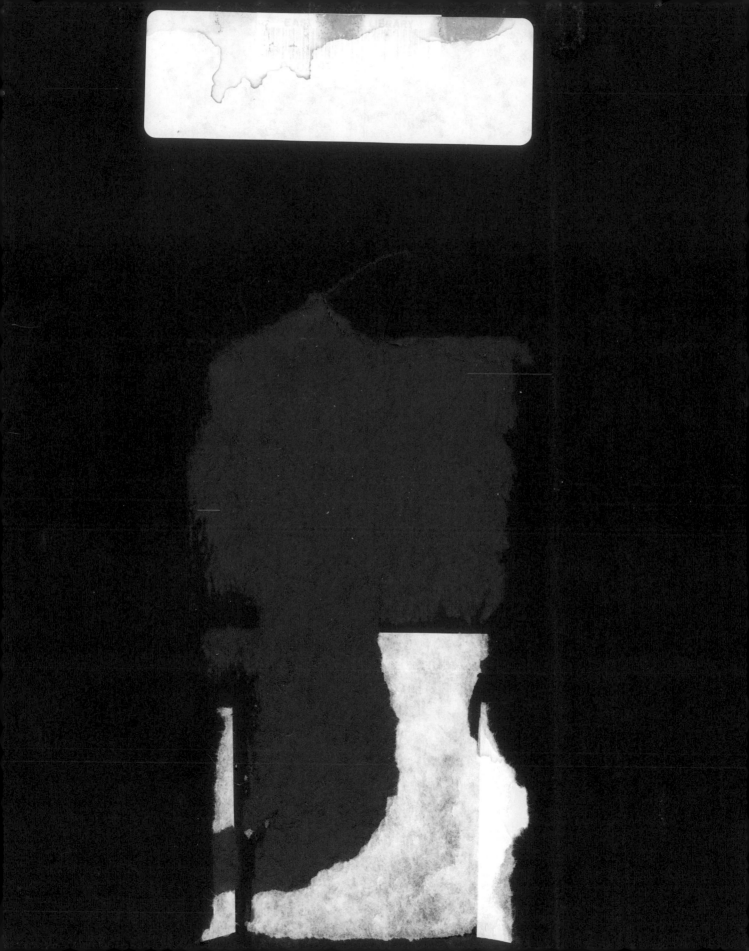